The Happy Life Story

Saving abandoned children on the streets of Nairobi

Sharon Emecz

Edited by Steve Emecz

Paperback ISBN 978-1-78092-749-7
ePub ISBN 978-1-78092-750-3
PDF ISBN 978-1-78092-751-0
Published in the UK by MX Publishing
335 Princess Park Manor, Royal Drive, London, N11 3GX
www.mxpublishing.com

Cover design by www.staunch.com

Contents

Happy Life

Happy Life is a children's home in the suburb of Kasarani in the capital city of Kenya, Nairobi. They rescue abandoned children from the streets, some of whom are orphans. There are around forty children aged 0-3 years at the main home in Kasarani. The organisation has also expanded out into Juja Farm (a small village near Juja, North of Nairobi) with another home with sixty children aged 3-11 years, a church and a school.

The mission statement is:

"Providing the abandoned children of Kenya with a home and hope for adoption"

Introduction

Chiumbo is nearing the end of his ten hour shift collecting garbage in the Kibera slum and he is exhausted. He's about to throw a clutch of carrier bags onto the wagon when he hears a noise.

He pauses – there is the sound again, coming from one of the plastic bags. He carefully lifts the rubbish from on top of what he can now see is a baby boy whose cries are growing faint.

Wrapped around the tiny infant's bruised neck is a piece of rope where it looks like he has been strangled, and the placenta is still attached. Chiumbo calls over one of the other collectors. "Mtoto (infant)" says Chiumbo. Carefully they unwind the rope and Chiumbo grabs a cloth from the truck and wraps the baby in it. An hour later and the baby is at the hospital and a call is made to one of the many children's homes in the area.

This scene is one that is played out many times a day, dozens of times a week and hundreds of times a month.

This book tells the story of Happy Life, one of the amazing organisations making a difference to the lives of abandoned children in Nairobi.

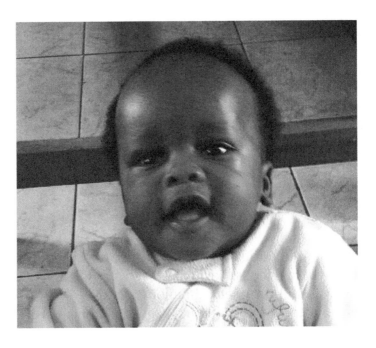

Beniah
[his name means 'God Builds']

Beniah is the young baby in the story above. He's a very affectionate baby and is still at Happy Life in Kasarani happy and healthy.

How This Book Came About

This book tells the story of one special children's home - 'Happy Life' based in the Kasarani suburb of Kenya's capital city Nairobi.

The story is told by Sharon Emecz, who after twenty years on the corporate treadmill in the UK took a career break and ended up at the Happy Life rescue centre. Sharon describes the impact that the experience has had;

> *[Sharon] Many people use the phrase 'life changing' when they have volunteered in areas with high levels of poverty but for me personally, that's the wrong term. A better way of describing what happened to me is 'perspective changing'. Do I still live in London with my job and comfortable life? Yes. Am I more fundamentally grateful for the hand that life has dealt me? Absolutely. Do I have a better appreciation for the situation in places like Kasarani – I really hope so. To see what the team at Happy Life have achieved in such a short space of time has been wonderful – and to play a small part in that is very rewarding.*

Once I decided to take three months off work, I approached one of the international voluntary organisations VSO, who came up with a couple of options – one of which was Happy Life. I spent the month of January taking my TEFL (Teaching English as a Foreign Language) qualifications and headed to Kenya in February. As part of the trip I organized a game drive out into the safari parks of Kenya and Tanzania and finished off with a brief visit to Zanzibar. I'm a big advocate of combining some travel with volunteering. Kenya is such a beautiful place and I felt it was vital to see some of the country and wildlife.

[Sharon] The first visit to Happy Life was quite intensive as everything was new and having some travel at the end of my time in Africa worked extremely well. I visited some places that I may never have got to in my life and I'd encourage anyone to add something similar on to the end of their volunteering trip.

I was very keen to come back and also felt that the experience would be something that would appeal to my husband, Steve. I asked the team at Happy Life when would be the best time to come back to bring my husband, and they immediately suggested Christmas;

[Sharon] It's obvious when you think about it, but many charitable organisations struggle to get volunteers over the Christmas holiday period – understandable as most people will spend that time with their families. So I took Steve for three weeks over Christmas and New Year 2013.

Volunteering together was an opportunity that Steve jumped at;

[Steve] I'd heard all about Happy Life from Sharon, and having travelled quite widely in the

developing world including India, Bangladesh and South America, I thought I'd take the conditions in my stride - I didn't. The word that comes to mind for me most is 'humbling'. Losing electricity and running water for days at a time was totally alien to me, but everyday life for the kids in the rescue centre. I hadn't come across a happier bunch of kids in my life. Those everyday things, like cancelled trains that used to wind me up, just seem so trivial when you see what these kids have been through, and what they deal with on a daily basis.

As soon as we arrived back in the UK, we booked our plane tickets for the next year. We were also keen to find a way to do something ongoing to create some sources of income all year round. We came up with the idea for the book and also began weaving some fundraising into our charity work with our publishing company and into the events we run through the year.

The final edits to this book took place in December 2014 when we returned to Happy Life.

Happy Life Kasarani

Happy Life Juja Farm

Kenya

[Sharon] In this chapter I take a brief look at the country as a whole, the economy, then drill down to get to know the area surrounding Happy Life.

Nestled on the coast of Africa, Kenya is a country of great contrasts. On the one hand it's one of the most important economies in the region, on the other it is the home to huge amounts of poverty. The majority of visitors to Kenya either come for business to the capital city of Nairobi, or for tourism to the coastal resorts like Mombasa. It is, however, the wildlife that draws the most visitors with some of the world's most stunning safaris.

A rhino in the wild (from my safari photos)

From the Masai Mara to Amboseli, Kenya has incredible scenery and wildlife.

Economy

[Sharon] Next I take a look at Kenya's economy.

According to the World Bank, Kenya has a population of just over 44 million, with around 46% of the population living below the poverty line. Three-quarters of the population are employed in the agriculture sector. About half of the production is subsistence, the rest goes for export with tea, coffee, corn and wheat as the main items.

Since its independence in 1963 (the country recently celebrated the 50th anniversary), Kenya has become a hub of economic activity for sub-Saharan Africa with Nairobi becoming the main financial capital. The Nairobi Stock Exchange (NSE) is the fourth largest in Africa. Investment into the country has increasingly come in recent years from China and Russia.

Nairobi Skyline (source: Shutterstock)

The services sector contributes over 60% of the country's Gross Domestic Product (GDP) and is dominated by tourism.

It is one of the most important economies in Africa and, apart from several dips due to terrorist activity, has shown good economic growth. It is the fourth largest economy in Africa behind Nigeria, South Africa and Angola.

According to the World Bank, economic output is around 4.76 trillion shillings ($53.1bn; £32.8bn).

> *[Sharon] Not long after my first visit to Happy Life the country went through national elections. The previous elections five years before had been very volatile – with much violence and many deaths. The elections this time went off relatively peacefully. There was a real sense of hope that Kenya had entered a new era. A new government that had pledged to reduce corruption and build a brighter tomorrow.*

Within a few months things had taken a much worse turn with the biggest impact on Kenya's economy coming in the form of terrorism.

In September 2013 the world watched in horror as a group of terrorists took control of the Westgate shopping mall in Nairobi and killed at least 67 men, women and children. It was the worst terrorist attack for more than a decade in Kenya.

Responsibility for the attack was claimed by the Militant Islamist group al-Shabaab from Somalia. (The attack was linked to the Kenyan Military's participation in African troop deployments in Somalia).

The impact on the country's tourism was prolific with hundreds of thousands of people left jobless.

Nine months after the Westgate attack, and just as it appeared that the economy and tourism had begun to turn around, a new series of attacks happened. This time the terrorists targeted local Kenyans with attacks in Eastleigh and Pangani in Nairobi. In May 2014 there were two bus bombings on the Thika Highway outside a hotel and at an underpass not far from Kasarani.

[Sharon] All conflicts and terrorism are awful but the incidents in Kenya are particularly saddening as this is such a warm and giving people.. The average Kenyan has no idea what's going on in Somalia – they are just trying to deal with the basics of life.

Dec 2014 Update

The Foreign and Commonwealth Office (FCO) advice in December 2014 was to avoid areas within 60km of the border with Somalia. This also applies for some areas in Nairobi including the suburb of Eastleigh which has a high Somalian population. The warnings have meant the numbers of visitors to Kenya have gone down. Fewer volunteers have been coming to organisations like Happy Life. However, we feel just as safe in Kasarani this year as we did last time.

Nairobi

Despite it's quite cruel nick name of 'Nai-Robbery' amongst tourism groups, as long as the traveler is careful, it is a relatively safe city to explore and enjoy.

There are some amazing places to go in Nairobi and two key places to visit have to be the Giraffe Centre and the Elephant Orphanage.

Elephants (from my safari photos)

Nairobi owes its existence to the East Africa railway. It was a depot along the route to Kampala, Uganda. After independence, Nairobi grew significantly resulting in the large slum areas. Primarily this is due to young Kenyans leaving their rural homes in search of jobs. Most are unable to find work and rather than return to their rural villages they choose to live in the slums. Today the city is reinventing itself as the economic hub of not only Kenya, but also Eastern Africa.

Our personal favourite place to visit in Nairobi has to be the Langata Giraffe Centre (Koitobos Rd) where they raise giraffes. You can visit the centre and go up onto a raised platform and meet the giraffes. If you are bold enough, you can try a 'Giraffe Kiss' by holding some food in between your lips so they can come get it. Great fun and amazing to see how affectionate these lovely creatures are.

I get a 'Giraffe Kiss' at giraffe centre

We would also recommend visiting at the same time the David Sheldrick Wildlife Trust, which looks after orphaned elephants. Around eleven o'clock you can watch the feeding of the baby elephants.

Kasarani

[Sharon] Kasarani is the home of the main Happy Life rescue centre and the place where I have stayed on each of my visits.

Located in the North of Nairobi is the suburb of Kasarani. You can reach it easily as it sits about 10km North on the new Thika Highway – a huge six lane road that was built by the Chinese (as many large infrastructure projects in Kenya are). To say it's a place of vast contrasts doesn't do the phrase justice.

Kasarani – the road in,
Happy Life is just off to the right

Kasarani is a mix of shacks, apartment buildings and a bustling commercial centre. The national football stadium and the Moi International Sports Centre sit on one side of the highway and on the other the stunning five star Safari Park Hotel. Right in between the two is a ramshackle market that snakes through the underpass.

A new mall was built in the last few years called the Thika Road Mall (TRM) near to the underpass and the Roysambu bus terminus.

The population is an estimated 200,000+ and it is thought that the name comes from a river that runs through the area and has the Kikuyu name Gathara-ini River.

Although a bit unsettling for unexperienced travelers, within a few days even first time volunteers have felt at ease. The people of Kenya are very friendly and speak English.

[Sharon] In the three weeks we spent at Happy Life we only saw a couple of Europeans in Kasarani. The only non-locals are aid workers and volunteers in the neighbourhood. You feel perfectly safe during the day as the locals know why you are there.

Kasarani

The Slums

[Sharon] During my first time at Happy Life I spent a day in the slum at Kibera visiting some of the schools and children's homes. It was an eye-opening insight into one of the poorest areas of Kenya that is very difficult to describe.

Many of the children that end up in Happy Life come from the slum dwellings of Nairobi. There are around 2.5 million people in the settlements in Nairobi. That makes up nearly 60% of the population.

The Nairobi Slums (Source: Shutterstock)

Kibera

The population of Kibera is nearly 1m. This makes Kibera Africa's largest slum and one of the world's biggest.

Kibera (Source: Shutterstock)

Some quick statistics about Kibera:

- The government owns all the land
- The average shack size is 12x12 feet
- The average number of people per shack is about eight, with most sleeping on the floor
- About 20% of Kibera has electricity
- The average monthly rent is about 700KSH ($10)
- The dwellings are mud walls with corrugated iron roofs
- Until recently Kibera had no water and it had to be collected from the nearby dam, which is very polluted with garbage and raw sewage. Now there are two mains water pipes into Kibera

- There are few toilet facilities with one latrine being shared amongst around fifty people
- There are no government hospitals or clinics, those that are there are provided by NGOs and churches
- One of the biggest challenges in Kibera is *'Changaa'* – an extremely cheap alcohol which at 50% proof, and with high levels of methanol, gets people very drunk very fast and is responsible for a lot of lawlessness
- Cheap drugs and glue are also a problem
- The unemployment level is around 50%

Kibera – (Source: Shutterstock)

The pregnancy level is extremely high with at any one time about 50% of 16 to 25 year old girls pregnant. Abortion rates are high and dangerous. Many of the NGOs are targeting this problem.

The Happy Life Story – How it started.

There are two couples at the heart of Happy Life – Sharon and Jim, and Faith and Peter. One from Delaware (USA), the other from Nairobi.

Left to right Jim, Sharon, Peter and Faith.

From Delaware – Jim and Sharon

Meet Sharon and Jim Powell. They live in Delaware and have been married thirty five years. They have four children, three boys and a girl. Jim taught in a Christian school for twenty years and was a pastor for twelve years.

While a pastor in Delaware Jim was on a men's retreat in the Poconos of PA along with a Kenyan Steve Kamau who had recently come over to the US. While walking together along a dirt trail in the woods they came up with the idea to set up a program in Kenya for abandoned children.

That was the beginning in the fall of 2000. After getting approval from the church in Delaware to have them start as the nonprofit organization, the three of them went to Kenya in the summer of 2001. Plans were made and Happy Life took in their first four kids in January 2002.

Pastor Peter, (Steve's brother) and his wife Faith have directed the home from the very beginning. Among themselves they reasoned that they could start with 4-5 kids and that if for some reason the ministry did not take off they could care for the 4-5 kids themselves. Well, it did take off and they have taken in well over 330 abandoned children with 170 (more than 50%) becoming adopted.

The adoption process in Kenya and the US has many similarities as to working with an approved agency and home studies. The big difference is that Kenya requires an international couple to be able to live in Kenya for at least 6 months (not required to have both parents all the time). This has had great limitation on most from the US. There are a number of countries in northern Europe where the governments are very supportive as to costs and job security. It is from these countries where most of the international adoptions have occurred. It has been very encouraging that Kenyans are now adopting the children and represent the majority of the adoptions.

Sharon and Jim have not adopted but have always seen adoption as something very good to do. Prior to meeting Steve, Sharon and Jim had no inclination to become directly involved with an adoptive ministry in Kenya.

Happy Life has been organized with a local church 'Overcoming Faith Ministry' being the owners and operators of the ministry. Whilst the US Board is advisory and supportive, Sharon and Jim believed from the beginning that, if the ministry would be self-sustaining, the leadership would have to be by Kenyans.

We asked Jim if he would do anything differently.

"Good question, that at first is difficult to answer. Even after I have thought about it for a few minutes no response comes to mind. From the very beginning one of our motivational verses has been Psalm 127:1 (paraphrased)

"Unless the Lord builds the ministry the builders' labor in vain. Unless the Lord watches over the ministry the watchmen stand guard in vain".

Since inception the Lord has provided great unity between those on the Kenyan Board and those on the US board. This has especially been true for the unity between Pastor Peter and myself. This is a huge praise in that it is often very difficult to have a work between the US and

Africa go so smoothly with one mind and one heart. We encourage people around the world to come and volunteer for an hour or 6 months. We have 4 guest quarters at the Nairobi property and will have some at the Juja Property."

*Peter, Faith, Sharon and Jim at
Kasarani Happy Life*

How often do you visit Happy Life these days?

> *"We go once a year to visit and each time we have been encouraged by the growth and vitality of the ministry. It's especially rewarding to meet the volunteers from around the world. We not only welcome volunteers we also consider them essential to the overall welfare of the ministry. Happy Life could not be where it is today without the volunteers."*

What are the costs of Happy Life and who are the main supporters?

> *"We are always looking for donor partners, churches and organizations who will donate to the ministry. Currently we have about 95 kids aged 1 week to 11 years. The costs for the complete operation of the ministry comes to about $150 a child/month. The Lord has blessed in the past 13 years with extra contributions that have enabled us to construct the buildings and purchase the properties. As the ministry grows we anticipate the future needs for building expansion. "*

From Nairobi - Peter and Faith

How many children are you caring for at the moment?

93 across the two. 35 in Juja, 58 in Happy Life. [in December 2014 this is now 102]

Is there an even split between boys and girls?

A few more boys. Boys seem to be abandoned more often than girls and girls are adopted more quickly.

In the last few months where have the children been abandoned?

Mainly in the local neighbourhoods, with most coming from the slums. Kibera, Mathare North, and low income areas, and in around Kasarani. The main reasons are poverty, HIV AIDS, and teenage pregnancy. We've been here 11 and a half years in this location so the local organisations, like the police and the children's department, know where we are.

What's the average time a child spends at Happy Life / Juja Farm?

Most people choose to adopt below one year. It seems like we have a fair amount of adoptions of children above a year. Since Happy Life is the guardian of the adoptable children, we are committed to care for them until they become adults.

How many children have been adopted so far?

170+

How did you end up choosing this location?

We were first renting a home 5 miles down the road and we had to move due to it being sold. Quickly we located to the current property with ¼ acre of land. After a year we asked the owner if he could sell. A lady in Delaware left in her will $15k – which we used as a down-payment on the $70k value. He gave us time to pay the rest. We soon raised the funds for a four story building which was completed in 2007.

How many permanent staff do you have?

33 permanent. 3 days on, 3 days night, 1 day off. 10 in Juja. 2-3 volunteers per month.

Where does the funding come from?

Happy Life receives donations from churches, individuals, families and businesses. Foundations provide some with grants, but there is no specific support from the government.

Where do most foreign volunteers come from?

> *From all over the world. USA, quite a few from Europe, Asia – but the majority of volunteers are from Kenya with many coming from the two local universities.*

How many foreign volunteers do you have each year?

> *2-3 per month.*

What skills do the volunteers bring and how does that help?

> *They spend time with the children, playing, giving them love which also helps free up the time for the care givers. They also help the 'mothers' with tasks, especially feeding.*

Are there any skills you are particularly looking for?

> *Teaching and nursing, construction, painting.*

Tell us about the school project at Juja Farm and how can people help with the school?

> *The focus of the school is to be a Christian school, and to involve children from the local community – Juja is a needy community so our school is there for our kids and also the local. We need books especially 'Beka' books which sit nicely alongside the Kenyan curriculum. Uniforms for the children – from shoes to*

everything else oh and stationery. Teachers will teach Swahili – but all the other subjects are in English. We're trying to set up computer rooms. Music and sports equipment – we have a sports area for the school – we have a large enough compound for soccer, basketball.

You describe Happy Life as a children's home?

We (Peter and Faith) like to say we're not an orphanage – we rescue, care and give up for adoption. We promote the importance of growing up in society rather than an institution.

How did the ministry for caring for abandoned children start?

We have been in church ministry so were used to helping with children from the poor and needy. The ministry started with Reverend Steve from the USA. He found a child that had been abandoned in the rain and was nearly drowning. He took the baby to the hospital. He shared his burden and brought with him Rev Jim Powell (and wife Sharon) and started talking about how they could help such children. Back then there were many street children – they decided to start with the babies.

The ministry started by renting a home and brought in twin boys that were found on the streets of Nairobi in a plastic bag – 3 days old. Then came a baby girl (abandoned in a hair salon). We said that even if it's just five children – we should do that. Faith was pregnant with twins at the time. We took the house because it was cheap. It was really nice, but built on a very rough road. People donated all the things for the house. It all started there.

What challenges were faced early on in setting up the adoption process?

In 2002 it was very tough. The 2003 Children's Act began to streamline the process. The first adoption was by a lady who was in the church in the USA with Jim. She heard about two of the children who were twins, and took the two boys after 3 months living here. We came to know of a lawyer who took us through step by step with the adoption process. Back then there were no established adoption agencies. Deborah lived in our house. Finally she got all the paperwork and visas. Even at the final step there were problems. We said goodbye and she went to the airport. We got a call from the airport, that they wouldn't let her on the plane as she had only one ticket for the two babies! It eventually got sorted out.

Where do the adoptive parents come from?

Most of the adoptions now are by Kenyans. Of the international ones, most of have been white families. The process is very long for the USA. Prospective parents have to spend at least six months in Kenya. One couple came here in July, left the following July – it took a whole twelve months. It's very tough for people to be away from their jobs. For missionaries and people in Foreign Service who have to be here for a year or two it's easier.

How did the process evolve?

The Children's Act made it much clearer. The adoption agencies are now more established. There are good quality agencies now and the social workers. Our administrators work with the agencies. Both also work with the courts.

Are there any other similar projects in Nairobi?

Quite a few. Still not enough. There are about 2.4m orphans in Kenya. 40m people in Kenya. The majority are not in a children's home – living in with families or on the streets.

What's special about Happy Life and Juja Farm?

The high quality of care – the children are happy and taken care of. There is a nurse on the ground all the time. Lots of mothers to ensure feeding, changing, bathing. We clearly follow the government policies. We are very careful with the care givers that we employ. There are very strong Christian values. Older children go to church on Sundays. There is also Children's Bible Club (200 kids) for four days.

What is the average diet for the children?

> *Rice and maize flour, chapatti, beans, and vegetables. We grow vegetables at Juja Farm.*

On my first morning I was woken by the sound of a cow. Can you tell us a bit about her?

> *She's our Biogas Cow – we dug a deep hole, built a tank that collects the manure. When it's covered up it decomposes, produces methane. That's then compressed – and piped into the building. It provides our cooking gas.*

Biogas Cow has now been joined by a second cow. Add two goats and you have quite an interesting set of farmyard noises to wake up to.

What are your plans for 2014 and 2015?

Expanding Juja. Incorporating the children from the local community. Building four classes of age kindergarten up to class 2 primary school. The capacity would be around 30 per class. We plan to have two streams that would in a few years' time increase up to perhaps 500 in total.

What support do you get from local businesses?

Supermarkets and shops bring foodstuffs – but generally that happens only at Christmas and Easter. During the year it is mostly from churches. We use brochures and the radio etc. - lots through the churches. We also have an annual fundraising walk which raises funds. Companies in Kenya choose a charity for the year. Some will do for just a year.

Annual fundraising walk

The Administrators

The administrators at Happy Life make sure everything runs as smoothly as possible - an incredibly tough and complicated job. The staff at Kasarani for our first visit were Rosemary, Joyce, Judy and Winnie. For our latest visit Liuba and Sarah have replaced Judy and Winnie. Here Rosemary talks about the administrator's role;

How long have you been at Happy Life?

> *Nearly ten years. I started visiting the children. I knew Peter and Faith as I visited the same church as them.*

And you've been looking after everybody here ever since?

> *Yes, it has been really hard work because when I came here we only had to feed five children, and now we have 93. We only had one ranch house, and the children were all squeezed in it in that small house, but I've seen real growth. Happy Life has been really helpful you know, I have seen so many things.*

It's been a real experience?

> *Yes, a great experience. I have seen so many children who have come and you are like "will they even make it to tomorrow?" But now they are big children; they are five, seven, eight years.*

And so, it has really helped me also to grow and to look at the world in another way.

What are your biggest challenges running Happy Life?

One of the biggest challenges is the help with the health of the children - it has never been easy when the children are sick. We have to go the hospital, get the drugs, you know. And, at the same time, the bills, the hospital bills, they're sometimes very high, so that's a big challenge. And it has always been like that since I came here. Yes, I think it's the biggest challenge.

Another challenge is that many of the children who come here are very young. Most of them are abandoned at night. If they are not left at the hospital they'll be abandoned at night on the streets you know?

Every time I've been to Happy Life there is always something happening on the medical front. There is an isolation ward for the sick children.

Because of the condition the children are found in do you have to take them to the hospital?

Yes. Depending on where some of them are left. Sometimes in the garbage or on wasteland so it is usually needed.

And do you use the main hospital in Nairobi?

> *We use different hospitals but we usually use Kenyatta hospital. The National hospital has become very expensive.*

Are there also medical centers?

> *Yes. But you know when you have a child who already has a problem, like they already have an illness that needs specialized treatment. You have to go to the hospitals.*

Do you get any discounts or anything from the hospital? Do you get any support?

> *No. There is only one hospital that helps. What they do is if a child is sick they can attend to the child and then they arrange so that we can pay later. Others have to be paid straight away. This hospital allows us to pay at the end of the month.*

What are your plans for 2014/15?

> *One of the things we are looking forward to is Happy Life Juja School. We need to get qualified teachers and make sure that our children get a good education.*

> *Here at Kasarani we are looking for what to do also for our younger children. One mother is taking care of 12 children. So we want to make*

sure that every month we have enough volunteers to help the caregivers.

So how many staff do you have in total across both locations?

We have 33 staff [with 10 at Juja] including caregivers, two security, the driver, four administrators, the nurse. Two of the caregivers are casuals.

What's the average day for the Administrator?

It starts around 8am. The first thing to do is to check in with everybody and get the reports from the night. If there were any children sick, what medicine they had and so on. Then it is on to the office work. We look at the tasks that need to be done and we split them up between the four of us. Things like taking children to the hospital, going to the bank, getting things from the shops.

If there is time for news, we update the blogs. With Jim being in the USA we have two time zones so it's always moving. We also have authors in Australia and Canada.

What time does the day finish?

Sometimes at five, but can be up to eight. On Thursdays I go out to Juja. When we have to take a child to the hospital everything stops. One time I had to run to the hospital and I didn't even get a chance to lock the office. When I went to the hospital I wanted to come back and lock up but they said no, this is serious you have to go with an ambulance and so we went in an ambulance to another hospital. We left at three in the morning. So, everything else collapses. You have to leave everything else.

Children having lunch at Juja Farm.
The multipurpose building is used for
many things from dining hall to church.

Juja Farm

With a never ending supply of abandoned children the team at Happy Life were keen to grow operations to provide more places.

With land prices and space becoming a premium in Kasarani, in order to expand Happy Life needed to find somewhere nearby that was suitable. About thirty minutes' drive up the Thika Highway is the bustling town of Juja. The town itself is expanding fast and presented a good mid-point to the village of Juja Farm. Land prices, due to the current lack of a tarmac road, were reasonable and that enabled Happy Life to purchase a few acres of land.

One of the goals with the 5 Acres of the Juja property was for the ministry to be also for the local community with a multi-purpose building and church open to locals. Two three room houses were built where the older children from Kasarani could live in a 'family' type setting.

The multi-purpose building

*When we visited in December 2013 the
first level of the school had been started*

The beginnings for an excellent Christian school were
underway.

The school will cater for up to 500 children

December 2014 Update

By the time we come to complete the book the school is not only up and running but also reaching out locally as Jim comments;

"We already have about 20 of the less privileged kids from the community be part of our school. There is also a church that meets for the community in our multipurpose building."

On the Juja property there are four 3-bedroom houses that are designed to have a "mom" living with 10-12 children. The goal being to give the children a sense of being part of a little family.

The new houses are already complete

Also on the Juja property there is the first floor of the education building with 4 classrooms. The team will construct a 2nd floor as the kids age and the numbers increase.

Peter at the first floor of the school where multiple classes are now up and running

The next project will be to construct and operate a clinic on the Juja property. There is a great need not only for Happy Life - 37 children have died from sickness in the past 13 years - but also for the surrounding community of Juja. Happy Life's children come usually from unknown parents with a variety of conditions/illnesses.

The Kids of Christmas 2013

Meet the kids from Kasarani Happy Life – 56 children from the Christmas and New Year 2013. It was our privilege to spend several happy weeks with these incredible children.

You won't find a happier bunch of kids. They have no possessions. Everything in the home is collective – from the clothes to the shoes, the books to the toys. That way nothing is wasted. No toys sitting in cupboards not being used, no clothes sitting on hangers in wardrobes. Stuff gets used here until it wears out.

Over the coming pages you'll meet some of the kids from Kasarani.

The babies from Infant A

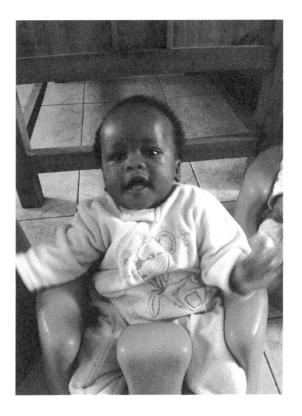

Beniah

2014 Update

Beniah is still at Happy Life in Kasarani. He was born on 11th September 2013 and rescued by garbage collectors a few blocks away from Happy Life. He was covered in blood, still joined to the placenta and had a rope around his neck.

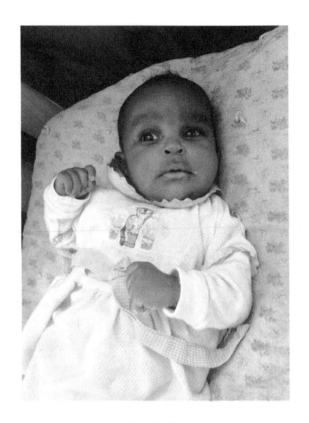

Daniella

2014 Update
Daniella and Gift [p 45] were adopted by a couple from UK who were then staying in Kenya. Daniella was born at Wendo hospital on 28th October 2013 and given up by her mother for adoption.

Elisha

2014 Update
Elisha was abandoned at Kahawa-West in the middle of the road. During 2014 Elisha got sick and died.

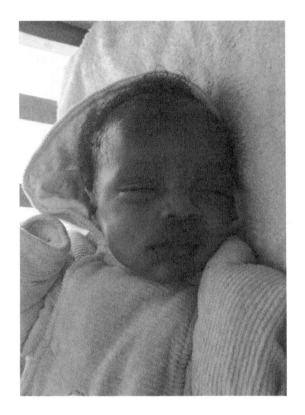

Gabrielle

2014 Update
Gabrielle was abandoned at Githurai near the Thika Road and was rescued by a good Samaritan. In 2014 she was reunited with her mother.

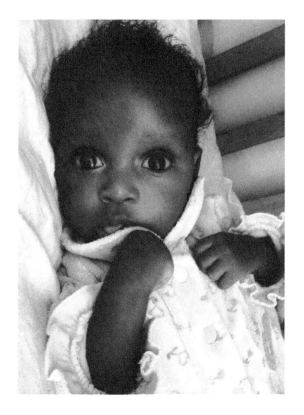

Gift

2014 Update
Daniella [p 42] and Gift were adopted by a couple from UK who were then staying in Kenya. Gift was born on 8th September 2013 and was given up for adoption through an agency the day after birth.

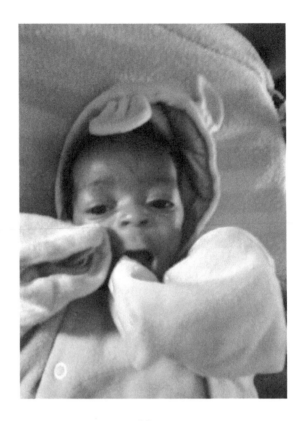

Liam

2014 Update

Liam was born on 20th October 2013 at Mbagathi hospital and abandoned by his relatives after his mother died of psychosis. Liam is still at Happy Life in Kasarani.

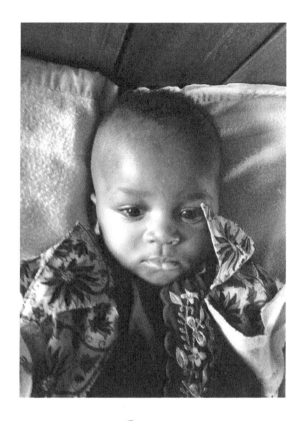

Samara

2014 Update
Samara was born premature on 31st May 2013 at Kenyatta hospital. In 2014 she was adopted by a single Kenyan Lady.

Tamara

2014 Update
Tamara was born on 9th June 2013 in Mbagatni hospital and given up for adoption there by her mother. Tamara is still at Happy Life in Kasarani.

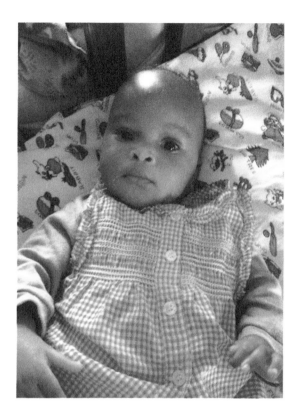

Trina

2014 Update

Trina was born premature on 25th May 2013 at Mbagathi hospital where she was abandoned. She was adopted two months ago by a couple who live and work in Kenya. The mother is from Tanzania and the father is from France.

Zahara

2014 Update
Zahara was born on 12th September 2013 and found abandoned along the main Mwiki-Kasarani road near Maji Mazuri. Zahara was adopted two months ago by a Kenyan family.

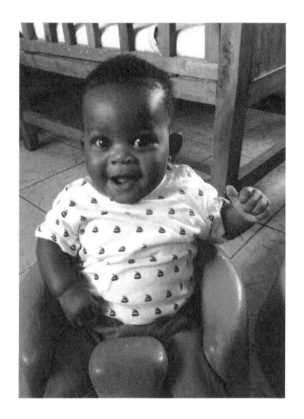

Zakai

We could have taken a hundred pictures of Zakai and each one would have him smiling. Have never ever seen a more smiley joyful baby.

2014 Update
Zakai was born on the 12th July 2013 and found near a river bank at about 7pm in the Zimmerman area by a good samaritan who rescued him. Zakai is still at Happy Life in Kasarani.

The Older Children

Leah and Trina

As we mention elsewhere in the book, one of the regular jobs every few hours is the baby feeding. One of the most heartening things was to see how the older kids get involved with feeding – especially at times when the resources are stretched.

To see a six year old youngster display such care and maturity is wonderful. It sounds like a small thing, but the regularity with which many of the older kids help out is quite astonishing.

Take Leah. She is feeding the babies and at six is quite happy to handle a shopping trip, organize the toddlers for lunchtime – but at the same time she's just a kid. Watching the switch between playing like a child and caring like an adult is wonderful.

2014 Update

Leah is still at Happy Life in Kasarani and continues to go to the local school. She enjoys school especially social studies but also maths. For some of the earlier older children like Leah, the team have decided to keep them in their local schools rather than move them out to Juja. With the more recent intake of children, once they reach school age they move out to Juja to free up vital space in the Kasarani home.

The older children like Leah, Loise, Charles, David and Freddy play a vital role helping out around Happy Life – from laundry to helping out with the smaller children.

The Toddlers

There are a couple of dozen toddlers at Kasarani and to say they are full of energy is an understatement. One of the important roles for the volunteers is to play with the kids and give a break to the mothers so that they can get on with others tasks.

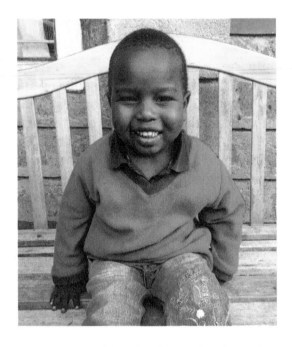

Surrounded by cheeky smiles (Isaac)

They split their time between their bedrooms and living room in the ranch house, and the small play area in the courtyard. The play area has a tented cover that's used to keep the sun off. At the back of the building, near the cows enclosure, is a small sandpit with a slide and a few swings. One of the favourite games for the children with the volunteers is hide and seek.

The first time Steve went to play with the kids they were absolutely fascinated by his light hair and hairy arms and legs – they had great fun pulling on his hair and climbing all over him.

The ranch-house with courtyard and the play area.

The Mothers

The 'mothers' are the staff that take 12 hours shifts to look after the children week in, week out. The majority have their own children so on top of running a household and looking after their own kids they are dedicating sixty plus hours a week to look after the children at Happy Life.

Hellen Njeri does not have children of her own and has worked at Happy Life for 6 years.

Phoebe Kibuthu is a mother of four children (two boys 20 and 15, and two girls 24 and 17). She's from Nyeri and came to Nairobi when she got married. She has been at Happy Life for 10 years and says "I feel really good when I am here. It's wonderful to be part of rescuing the kids".

Agnes Dinah - she is a mother of one and has worked at Happy Life for almost two years now.

The Foreign Volunteers

As the founders have mentioned, foreign volunteers play a vital role at Happy Life. When we returned in December 2014 we met Mike and Laura Archer (from Virginia, USA) who will spend a total of six months here at Happy Life Kasarani:

"We are Michael and Laura. Michael grew up in Kenya and spent 14 years calling Nairobi home. After we were married, we decided we wanted to spend some time together in Kenya, the country Michael loves so much. We searched for places to volunteer and found Happy Life Children's Home. We moved in on our 2 year wedding anniversary and have been spending our days with the beautiful children here at Happy Life."

Mike and Laura with the toddlers

Michael and Laura both have regular jobs but also work as wedding photographers and whilst they have been here they have helped update the website, especially with the format and the children's pictures.

Laura with Maxine

"We have so enjoyed getting to know all of the children, seeing our first rescued baby (Anthony) and today, seeing our first adoption (Violet), meeting Peter and Faith, being here while Jim and Sharon came to visit from the states, and meeting some other amazing volunteers."

Mike & Laura's Blog – https://archermwphoto.wordpress.com/

Volunteers at Happy Life come for anything from one week to several months. Some come back year after year. One such returning volunteer is Anna Thora from Reykjavik (Iceland). Anna first came to Happy Life in September 2013 and returned in August 2014. Christmas 2014 is her third visit.

We've seen Anna spend a lot of one to one time with the children. For example with Sophie to get her to try some different types of food. With Zakai to help him try to walk, and as of yesterday with the latest rescued baby 'Love' who came from the hospital very malnourished and tiny.

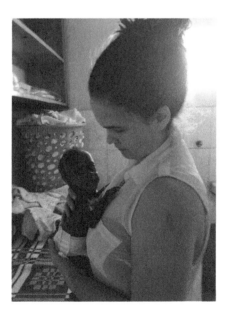

At four months 'Love' is the size and weight of a premature baby (just 1.9kg). He was abandoned at the hospital by his mother.

Fundraising

Funds for Happy Life come from a variety of sources. Some local businesses help out, the churches linked to Happy Life provide a lot of funds. There are many individual donors – it was one of those that helped the team buy the land out at Juja Farm – but one of the most important programs is the sponsorship of the children.

There are several levels of monthly sponsorship:

$30, $50, $100 and $200 (greater monthly amounts can be arranged)

It is important to bring new sponsors on board, as some will always be dropping off each year.

People can make one time donations or other monthly donations that are general towards Happy Life daily running expenses.

Funds for the operation and expansion of Happy Life come from a variety of sources;

- Individual and family donations.
- Various churches
- Foundations and grants
- Sponsorship of the children
- Various fundraisers

Main Projects

Here are the main projects over the past 13 years:

- Purchase of the Ranch house in Nairobi
- Building the 4-story building in Nairobi
- Purchase of 5 acres for Juja Campus
- Multi-purpose building at Juja Campus
- Well boring and installation   (Juja)
- Duplex 3-bedroom houses   (Juja)
- First floor of school building   (Juja)
- First floor of housing complex (Juja)

2015 Projects and Beyond

Three Story School Building:
- Classes for Preschool, kindergarten, classes 1-8, computer room.
- First floor of 4 classrooms completed in 2013
- Goal for 2015 is to complete the second floor
- Goal for future years will be to add the third floor. Another three story building will be needed for grades 9-12 as the children age.

Four Story Housing Unit:
- Each floor consists of two 3-bedroom houses
- First floor completed in 2014
  Goal for 2015 is to complete the second floor
- Goal for the future is to complete the 3rd and 4th floors to accommodate the children 3 years and older who have not yet been adopted.

Clinic:
- The concept of a clinic, especially for our children and for the needy children of the Juja Farm Community.
- Goal for 2015 is to perform extensive research in the type of clinic that will be best suited for Happy Life and the community. Construction will begin when the research is completed.

Washroom / Bathroom Facility:
- Goal for 2015 will include facilities for teachers and students

Future Projects:
- Dining Hall
- School Administration Building
- Guest Houses

The Adoption Process

2014 Update
It is with great disappointment that we report that the Kenyan government recently (Nov 2014) banned all foreign adoptions.

The adoption agencies are all lobbying for this to change as while the number of foreign adoptions is small (about 350-450 a year) it forms an important part of adoption in Kenya.

Our two case studies go into quite a lot of detail on the adoption process for those particular situations. What we've seen is that the process seemed to vary depending on the country that the adoptive parents are from.

Generally adopting from Kenya was a quite intensive and time consuming process for many countries, which many agree is not a bad thing. By the time the parents from UK, France, Germany and USA adopted a child from Kenya the chances of long term success are high as the safeguards ensuring that the parents and child bond were very good.

There are many public cases of countries where the adoption rules are not so stringent and rushed adoptions have resulted in bonding issues.

People quote a host of reasons for adopting from Africa. The need for adoptive parents is apparent, and the strong process and removal of corruption from the system in some countries like Kenya means that there's a high chance of success.

The final dimension is that you are going to be exposed to one of the most wonderful regions in the world. Kenyans are amongst the warmest and most welcoming we've come across, and we have travelled extensively between us. The countryside, and in particular the wildlife, are incredible. Adopting a child from the region means that this place is going to be a big part of your future and you will visit regularly to enable your child to reconnect with their heritage – a great chance to regularly visit this beautiful place.

Case Studies

To get a deeper understanding of the human part of the process, we worked with the Happy Life team to arrange a couple of interviews with adoptive parents. Whilst as we've mentioned, the majority are Kenyan, we wanted to talk to those that were perhaps a bit more unusual in the adoption process. So we decided upon one of the few foreign couples and a single mother.

The interviews were conducted over Skype and recorded using an iPhone to capture everything.

[Sharon] The interviews had to be one of the most fascinating parts of the process. We didn't know what to expect and both case studies introduced us to very interesting people - their obvious love for their adoptive children shone through as they talked passionately about how things played out for them.

Klaus and Karina

So Klaus, tell us a little about you and your family.

Well, my name is Klaus and my wife is Karina. We live about 50km away from Frankfurt in Germany. We've been married for about eight years.

Do you have any other children?

No. Our original plan was to have our own children and also adopt a baby from Africa. As it turned out, due to a medical condition we can't have our own children.

Tell us about your son?

His name is Dhomana. It's a D-H sounding like an English T-H and he is about two and a half years old. We got him in June.

Karina and Dhomana

You're talking to us from Kenya, so is that part of the process?

Yes. First of all both parents have to stay at least three months in the country for the foster period, then there is a court process after that which can take three or four months. After that you are officially the parents. So we are Dhomana's parents since Christmas when we then had to apply for his passport. This is a bit of a struggle with the German authorities and embassy and we're still in that process of trying to get a passport – so you have to think about staying for perhaps another half a year.

So what's he like?

[laugh] I'm glad you asked that. He is very much into gadgets. Smartphones, cameras, cars. I think if I would guess what he would be when he grows up now I would say a truck driver – either that or a comedian. He's either playing with cars or being a comedian – centre of attention.

Klaus, Karina and Dhomana

He likes to make people laugh, plays up?

Absolutely.

When did you first think about adoption?

We've been together about 16 years, but it was really when we got married and started thinking about children. We're both pretty open minded, and we knew about the situation In Africa. We'd travelled to Africa before and loved the places and the people and for us it was always the decision to have a black baby. If we could help one kid at least – that was always our goal to adopt an African child.

Did you ever think about adopting locally?

No. It was never our intention to adopt a German kid. I think it was always the thought we wanted to help an African child.

How did you come to choose Kenya?

I think that's the most common question we are asked. We wanted to adopt an African child, but we also wanted to do things according to the legal rules. I know there are other ways of doing things, if you are a celebrity like [names removed just in case for legal reasons]. With money you can do everything. We checked the processes of all the countries and there were only a few that had a proper process. The advantages for Kenya were quite a few. First of all the foster period. We liked the fact that you have to stay in the country with the kid for three months. This means that you get tight with the kid in his own country – there is not the double shock of new white parents and the new country with very different weather.

Second we knew that with Kenya there were many more children than adoptive parents or applicants, so there is a huge need. The third thing was for our own benefit as it is an English speaking country which makes it a lot easier. Finally Kenya is a great place to come back to – you know when he wants to see his origins. It's always great to come to Kenya and it's a great country from a nature perspective.

Had you been to Kenya before?

No, we had travelled to South Africa and several other countries but this was our first time in Kenya.

Talk us through the adoption process

I can only answer now from the German process, I don't know how that works in the UK. First you find the adoption agency that works with the Kenya authorities - and then step one is that you get approved as adoptive parents in your country. I think that's a step everyone has to take whether they are going for a domestic adoption or foreign adoption. That's step one. Step two is that you need to get approved by the Kenyan government, and for this you have to provide a huge bunch of documents to the Kenya authorities that took us, I would say, approximately half a year. You collect all the documents and get them certified then go to court and get them legalized. You then send them to the country. You then wait for the approval. So, collecting and sending documents to Kenya took half a year and then we waited for one year until they approved us. This took longer than normal because the company we were using was disbanded.

OK, in terms of the process, was it relatively easy getting approved as adoptive parents in your own country?

That was I would say, when I now look back [LAUGH], the easiest part yes. It still takes up to I'd say nine months to get the domestic approval. We'd go there for interviews or they have to collect paperwork for the German authorities and so that all in all it took is nine months. It wasn't that difficult let's say, but it was very time consuming.

Some eight weeks after we got approved we got the so called child proposal. I don't like the expression because it's not really a proposal. So we got the documents and a picture of him. There was a brief history to say where he was found, his medical condition, stuff like that. I think we had like three weeks' to think about whether we accept the proposal or not. We accepted I would say the next second.

Four weeks later we arrived in Kenya. We spoke to the Happy Life team and asked about him, what things to bring and how we could help him be a little bit better prepared.

Then we had one week bonding phase at Happy Life. So for the first seven days we went there on a daily basis, I'd say for eight hours or so. And spend the whole day with Dhomana. Like playing with him, feeding him, going to the restroom, changing diapers, stuff like that.

And then after one week we took him back home to our house in Nairobi, which we were renting. Then we have the three months fostering period as I explained before. After this we apply and wait for his passport – this taking three to four months. So overall we're now here for more than eight months.

So you will take him back to Frankfurt soon?

My wife already had to go back so I will follow in three to six weeks' time. I plan to take him on safari and down to Mombasa. I plan to have some fun with him here. Instead of sitting around and waiting.

Do you have some kind of open-ended visa?

No. It's a big issue really. They say that the adoption process can take at least six months. At the same time, the Kenyans let you stay for a maximum of six months. So it makes absolutely no sense. In my case I went back to Germany twice. Every time I re-enter Kenya I get a new three month visa. It's not that bad a situation – I mean I am backwards and forwards but each time I just buy a new visa.

What general advice would you give to adoptive parents?

What some people don't realise is that their responsibilities are just like any other parenting, ultimately they have all those responsibilities and it's not just about adoption, it's about being a parent long into the future. In our case the one element that's different is the fact, that at two years old our son already has his own mind – something that's hard to understand unless you are in the same position.

The main positive thing I would advise is don't think about it too much. In a sense, what could I do wrong? One of the questions we asked ourselves is 'Can we love this kid?' Don't think about it, you will love him. I never met an adoptive parent that didn't. 'Can I accept him as my son?', I mean he's not mine from a biological sense. This is complete nonsense and during the initial period you will fall in love for sure – 100%. There's no doubt about this.

If you really want kids then go ahead. Trust and follow your heart.

One more piece of advice that came from the German adoption agency - it's important that you don't just do this to help a child out. There's two sides to this and you have to be ready to have a kid, raise a kid, not just adopt to help poor child get out of their situation.

Have you been back to Happy Life with Dhomana?

Yes [laugh]. They were really shocked. In that time he'd grown ten centimeters and gained some weight. He had changed completely – he speaks German for one thing. He's caught up very fast. After eight months his character has developed a lot. He's changed dramatically, honestly dramatically and this is for all kids I know from adoptive parents.

You ask him 'have you been to school' and he thinks about it and then he shares everything with everybody all of a sudden. It is like me and when it comes to eating, my wife is a vegetarian and he's I would say 95% vegetarian. So somehow he's like us, more and more like us in every way. He changed really a lot. He's not the same kid like in the beginning. That's really, completely amazing.

What has been the reaction of friends and family?

I would say that the vast majority like the idea. I would say the younger the people are, the more positive the reaction is. Some people, especially older people, were a bit I would say, reserved. The real reaction comes later maybe. Some people are skeptical because he will run into trouble. But basically nearly everybody has a deep respect for what we do and like the idea of what we are doing.

A funny story is that of my mother. In the beginning she was very reserved and I think she didn't really like the idea. She never said so, but it was my gut feeling. And she was here in November for two weeks to see him. And so she came to Kenya and immediately fell in love. She even got herself an iPad so she can skype [laugh].

I remember, our pastor who was here three times and who wrote a report about us which he had to show to the church. I remember that he asked us about race, and we answered that my wife and I don't see the colour anymore. I don't see the black colour, I see this face. But I don't see the colour. This is, I think only something you can understand when you fall in love like my mom did.

For some people it is part of the reaction. Of my older brother, for example, or my mother, or my dad-in-law that they ask us 'are we really sure'. My dad-in-law asks us why don't you go for a Russian kid? Or a German kid? Or a Polish kid? They are white. We said, no. But basically, a very positive reaction, I would say. Very positive.

[Sharon] One of the difficult things writing this book is to get across in writing the love for Dhamona that Klaus obviously has. It was a fantastic forty-five minutes interviewing him and there's more than we're able to capture here. What struck us both was how we'd heard of the change of people's reaction, within the adoptive parents' support network – between before and after they met Dhamona. This is something we hear a lot about at Happy Life. Friends and family's initial reaction is difficult for them to form properly as the concept of a black baby for a white couple is unusual for them to understand. But like Klaus's mother, all it took was for her to meet him and see the love that had her son had for this baby boy and that changed in an instant.

Dhomana

You can watch the video of how Dhomana and another baby Ezekiel were rescued:
http://youtu.be/9qrDOlV6DqA

The Single Mother

So, tell us a little bit about yourself?

My name is Mary and I work for the United Nations. We have a mobility clause whereby we move around every three, four or six years. I'm a single mom and I have an eight year old daughter called Teona.

A couple of years ago I adopted Patience from Happy Life. So now I have two daughters.

Teona's eight and I talked to her about Patience - about having a baby sister and as a single mom I realised that it was going to be tough. There were also issues to do with her father. But we spoke about that and then we prayed about getting a small sister. So she's been very positive.

So Teona has adapted well?

Yes she's been very positive and I would say very gracious towards Patience and very welcoming. I think it was the fact we were in Ethiopia at the time where adoption is very common. If I was not in Ethiopia, I wouldn't have considered adoption.

Tell us about Patience.

Her name since she was born was Patience. So we call her Patience. I was told at Happy Life that she was left in the outpatients department of a hospital in Nairobi, and she was taken to the children's part of the hospital and after two months that's when she was taken to Happy Life.

Now she couldn't be put up for adoption because her papers were not available. This is why she stayed in the home until she was four and a half years old. I remember the day I met her. It was a long story but I was becoming desperate. I was in another country, I wanted a bigger child and I couldn't get a bigger child. And then one day, I was taken to Happy Life by a social worker from another children's home, and little Patience came singing oblivious to everybody around. You know she has this very sweet smile and very keen eyes, the kind of child you look at twice. We started to talk and we bonded.

I had this feeling that 'she's the one'. She can talk Swahili and we were singing some Swahili songs so I would say that part of it was kind of easy. It was just this thing. I saw Patience singing and she wasn't aware that any one was looking at her. And I wasn't aware that all the other ones were looking at me to see how I was reacting.

How long did things take to settle down?

It took three weeks to get accustomed to each other and eventually she came home. It's very interesting, I have seen her change. She didn't speak any English then and she speaks perfect English now.

She's very smart. I have to thank God for that. She is among the top of her class and she grasps things very, very fast. She's very motivated and she is the best reader in her class. Last night my older daughter was telling me that Patience was called two grades higher to go and read to the older children because she can read so fluently.

What I'm saying is I think it's a sign. I know that Happy Life really tries to give the best care for the children - especially on nutrition. Patience is a testimony to that. She was well taken care of when she was young.

So how old is Patience now?

Patience just turned six. You know, we took the day when she was found in hospital to be her birthday because they say that then, she was newly born. So she just turned six on the 4th of February.

What things does she like to do best?

The first thing is she's curious. She observes and makes comments. You know she doesn't take anything for granted. You could be somewhere, and she makes a comment - it could be true, it could be embarrassing or uncomfortable. The other day a colleague of mine, he's bald. You know, he doesn't have hair. [laugh] So she asks him. Why don't you have hair? I have to explain to her that you don't ask like that.

We established the rules so she knows what I expect from her. She likes playing, she likes her sister, and they have a dog. She likes bathing the dog every week.

She plays with her sister and they read. The latest thing is picking out each other's teeth, you know. At eight and six, they help each other to take out one tooth a week because they want the Tooth Fairy to come.

Has she said what she wants to be when she grows up?

Right now she is influenced so much by her sister who wants to be a vet. On the other hand, I got her a piano teacher as she seems really keen on the music.

She's also said that she wants to be a teacher and has dolls and plays with them like a teacher. But you ask her near her sister and she wants to be a vet.

So you came across Happy Life through another children's home?

Yes. I came across Happy Life through a social worker from another children's home called The Nest, because you see I had a very specific situation. My job is as an international civil servant and I move around a lot. So I just thought I wanted an older child so that she could cope with a sister who was then five going to six. I was desperate because girls go very fast in Kenya.

I don't know if you know this story but boys do not move as fast as the girls for adoption. Because of some community myths, boys are not as sought after as girls so I expected to struggle to get a girl who is bigger.

Yes, we heard that as well, that the girl babies are adopted very quickly. When did you first think about adopting?

Well, mine is a long story. I trained as a social worker. That was my first degree back in the 90s. I actually worked in the first adoption agency in Kenya, Child Welfare Society of Kenya.

When I look back I say, 'I'm lucky to have this job that I have'. I try to bring up my other daughter well. I talked to my friends and they agreed and supported me.

Can you take us through the different reactions?

For me the first thing is I'm single and I have a relatively good job in Kenya. I'm working for the UN, and kind of a career woman.

The first reaction I got was 'why don't you have your own?' You had your own daughter why don't you have your own again? And that is what was confusing everybody. They were baffled as to why I would want to adopt. In my mind I knew what I wanted though.

There's this thing in Kenya about "my child, my blood, my family, my name". I mean there's kind of a stigma associated to adoption. So that was the first reaction.

Then the second thing was why? I mean, you never know what you are getting yourself into. There are these stories of kids who were adopted and the parents never know what the background is like.

Yes, I have money, but there is something bigger than that. Because when you adopt a child it's not about now. It's about the future. It's about giving somebody hope, a kind of spirituality related to the whole thing, because you have to have faith.

I have faith in Patience. From the day I saw her, I have faith in her. I believe in her, I believe in her despite her background.

[Sharon] Once again it's difficult to get across in the interview notes the passion that's in the voice of these adoptive parents. We're both business people for whom presenting, talking and getting our point across happens so often every day we forget we're even doing it.

Mary was very nervous during the interview – you may be able to tell in the repetition – but she was desperate to get her points across. How much Patience means in her life and how important the adoption process is.

The Future

Looking at the progress that Happy Life has made in the last two years there is little doubt that the number of children that will be saved and will get to have a family life will continue to grow.

In 2014 there have been twenty five new children rescued to Happy Life, and nineteen have been adopted.

A really big part of the progression of Happy Life is the addition of the school and seeing the pictures from the recent graduation group are heartwarming.

When we asked the team for the current projects they are a mix of big and small, ambitious and practical.

School Materials
- Building of the school kitchen
- Building of the school toilet block
- Purchasing the kitchen equipment and utensils
- Stationery and learning materials
- School playing materials e.g balls, ropes etc
- 8-4-4 text books (from baby class to class four)
- Black school shoes – (size 30 – 36)
- School uniforms (Boys and girls)

There are everyday items too that wear out and are always needed:

- Electric kettles
- Microwaves
- Blenders
- Cotton bed sheets (baby cots)
- Mosquito nets (squared, 4X6)
- Mattresses
- Gas cookers and cylinders
- Multivitamins

How You Can Help

There are many ways you can get involved and support Happy Life. The first is to share the news of what they are doing and encourage people to follow their Facebook page. You can sponsor a child which makes a huge difference.

You can donate via the Happy Life website:
http://www.happylifechildrenshome.com/

If you or your organization can help with any of the materials that Happy Life needs please get in touch.

And of course you can come and visit Happy Life and volunteer a week or three. You will find it incredibly rewarding.

Happy Life Kenya Tel: 00-254-723-024327
Pastor Peter – Director, Faith – Managing Director.
Email: ndungukamau@yahoo.com
Website: http://www.happylifechildrenshome.com/

Happy Life USA   Tel: 001- 302-229-2098
Pastor Jim – USA Director
Email: happylifechildrenshome@gmail.com

Please do 'like' the Facebook page –
https://m.facebook.com/happylifechildrenshome

Read the latest news on the blog -
http://happylifekenya.blogspot.com

Volunteering in Kenya

Most people that come to Kenya and other countries in the sub-Saharan region Africa do so through voluntary organisations in the first instance. This is a good starting point if you have no contacts, but if you are able to deal directly with a project then more of the money you spend goes directly to the project.

Agencies that connect volunteers with projects play a vital role, and they can help find the right project for you. However, we would encourage you to reach out to your friends and family to see if there are programs that they already know of and have checked out.

For Happy Life there is a volunteers manual:
http://happylifechildrenshome.com/volunteers-manual.html

Steve at feeding time with infant Joash

Acknowledgements

The list of people to thank is very long. Firstly to Peter and Faith, Rosemary and the whole team at Kasarani for making us so welcome. To my husband Steve for his support and enthusiasm and to Bob for his help with the book images and cover.

The biggest thank you goes to the children of Happy Life. They are an inspiration and have given me something very special in my life.

Sharon Emecz

Kickstarter

This book would not have been possible without the kind support of the backers of the Kickstarter project.

The website sponsors:

Phil Growick
https://www.facebook.com/philgrowicksherlockholmes

The English Sisters
http://www.englishsisters.com/

Staunch Design
http://www.staunch.com/

Scurri
http://www.scurri.co.uk/

Kieran Mcmullen, Emma Jones, Darren Heaphy, Paul Stephens, Jackie Wilkinson, Amanda Cooper, Bernadine Felle.

... and a big thank you to all the other contributors.

CPSIA information can be obtained at www.ICGtesting.com
Printed in the USA
BVOW10s1121230315

392818BV00001B/1/P